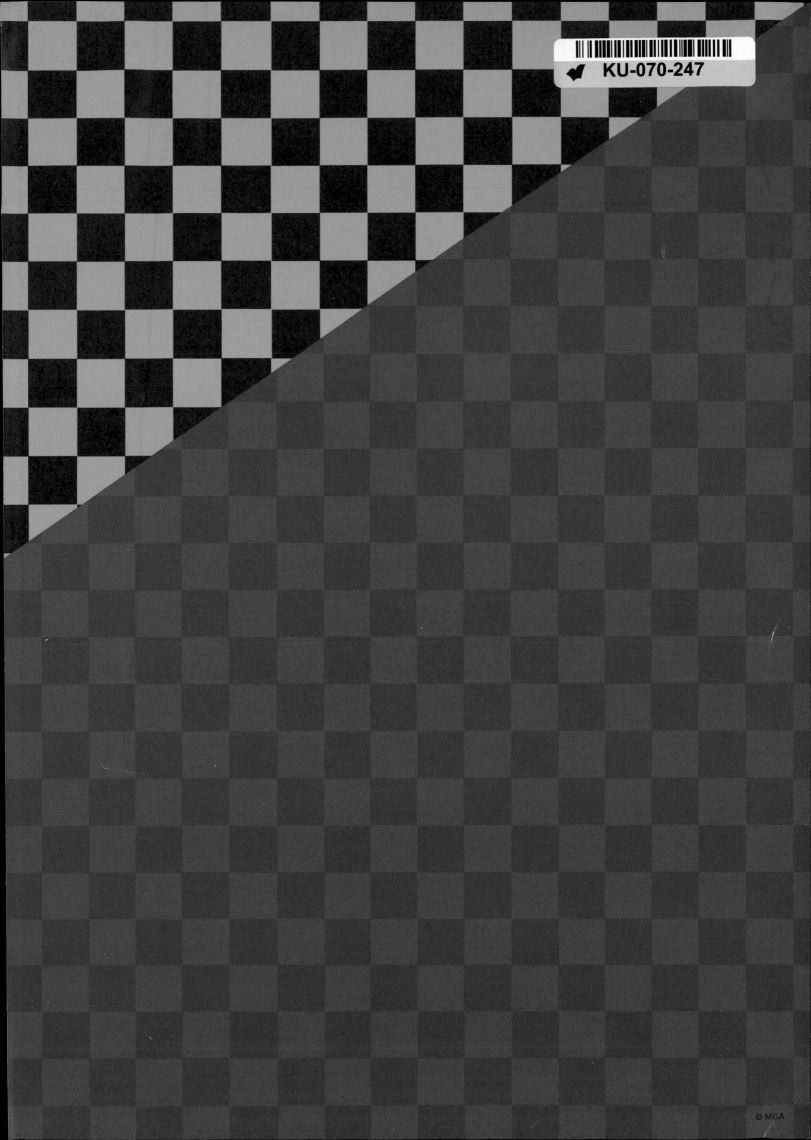

ALL THIS INSIDE!

Published 2020.
Little Brother Books Ltd, Ground Floor, 23 Southernhay East, Exeter, Devon EX1 1QL

books@littlebrotherbooks.co.uk
www.littlebrotherbooks.co.uk

Printed in Poland.

The Little Brother Books trademark, email and website addresses, are the sole and exclusive properties of Little Brother Books Limited.

© MGA

L.O.L. SURPRISE!
O.M.G.
OUTRAGEOUS MILLENNIAL GIRLS ™

THIS ANNUAL BELONGS TO

_____

_____

WELCOME TO THE WORLD

OF THE OUTRAGEOUS MILLENNIAL GIRLS!

Are you ready to SLAY THE RUNWAY?

Welcome to the fierce and fabulous world of the Outrageous Millennial Girls. This fantastic friendship crew eats, lives and breathes fashion, and they're here to bring you the latest trends, straight off the catwalk! It doesn't matter what your style is - it's how you strut your stuff that matters. So channel your inner diva, and let's go!

The Outrageous Millennial Girls are all about...

- ✔ SWAGGER
- ✔ Creativity
- ✔ Confidence
- ✔ Fashion
- ✔ Friendship
- ✔ TOTALLY BEING YOURSELF

O.M.G. SLAY THE RUNWAY!

Turn the page and let's get
FIERCE AND FABULOUS!

SPOTLIGHT ON...

Lady Diva

Big hair, big attitude!

Lady Diva was born to take the centre stage, and rocks every room, just by being there! She loves to sing, dance and speak her mind, and you can be sure you'll sit up and notice when she rolls into town! Her street style is totally fierce and 100% original. She loves bright, bold prints mixed with blinging accessories and a dazzling smile.

SIGNATURE STYLE:
Leopard print, big hair, street style.

MOST LIKELY TO...
Rock the show.

YOU'LL FIND HER...
Learning her lines and practising her tunes.

MOST KNOWN FOR:
Her amazing dance moves, her bold colours, her strut!

TRY BRINGING SOME LADY DIVA STYLE TO THESE SHOW-STOPPING PIECES.

TOPS

JACKETS

BOOTS

HOW TO... DAZZLE
EVERYDAY

Crystal Star is here with some tips to help u glow, girl!

FLASH UR PEARLIES

CONFIDENCE

Spend a little extra time brushing your teeth and you'll be amazed at the difference it can make to your smile! And when you smile confident, you'll feel confident too. So turn up the brushing and turn on the brightness!

DO: Brush your teeth for a minute longer than you usually do.

CHANNEL YOUR INNER CONFIDENCE

ENCOURAGE

Crank up a can-do attitude, and you'll get a glow that money can't buy! Everyone is good at some-thing, so whether you're super sporty, great at maths, or a brilliant friend, believe in yourself and don't afraid to show others what you're good at.

SAY: "I've got this, I can do it!"

DO SOMETHING FOR OTHERS

TEAM SPIRIT

Nothing gets a good glow on more than making someone else's day! So whether you're taking a few minutes to write a friend a special note, or taking a trip uptown to source that special accessory for a pal, doing things for others gets those feel good vibes buzzing!

DO: Be kind to someone else at least once a day

TRY SOMETHING NEW

PERSONAL DEVELOPMENT

Okay, trying new stuff can be a tricky business. It's so much easier to just stick with what you know. But get this: trying new stuff also makes you feel great, and puts a little bounce in your step! So if you're thinking of trying a new look, or maybe a new hobby, stop putting things off and just glow for it. You'll buzz with new focus and everyone will want to hear about your latest thrill!

DO: Find out about that new thing that you've always wanted to try.

POSITIVE PSYCHOLOGY

BE YOURSELF

Always be you, that's Crystal Star's every day mantra! Being true to yourself means that you'll al-ways be 100% sure that you're living every day in the best way. Trying to fit into someone else's idea of fun, can be fine for a while, but if it's not really for you, you'll always be feeling like there's some-thing missing. And guess what, being you is great! You'll draw people to you, because they can tell you're living your best life.

DO: Never stop being you!

GET YOUR ICE BREAKERS READY

ENCOURAGE

Sometimes, knowing what to say can be something that holds you back. Like, have you ever been in a room of new people, and been dying to join in, but you just can't do it? That's where you need to crack open your conversation ice breakers! If you think about what you want to say to people before you're in the moment, it will be a lot easier when the time comes.

SAY: Write down three ice-breakers and use them!

_____

_____

_____

WHAT'S YOUR
OUTRAGEOUS MILLENNIAL GIRL ALIAS?

Pick one word from the two lists to make your Outrageous Millennial Girl name.

Let's discover yours!

CUTE
GLOW
FIERCE
CHIC
UNIQUE

FRESHALICIOUS
MC SWEETIE
GENIUS
SWAG

MY OUTRAGEOUS MILLENNIAL GIRL NAME IS:

_____

© MGA

MAD SWAG

The Outrageous Millennial Girls are meeting to chat all things fashion.

Draw lines to match the close-ups to the correct spot in the picture.

©MGA

a.
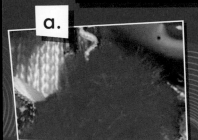

b.

c.

d.

e.

f.

g.

ANSWERS ON PAGE 76

13

SPOTLIGHT ON...

Candylicious

Sweet, with an extra TWIST

Candylicious is all about the pastel shades, and she mixes them together in a candy-coloured whirl! Everything she does has a cute little embellishment, and she carries her beloved plush bear with her at all times. Think manga to the max, with cartoon characters, sparkles, and prettiness galore.

SIGNATURE STYLE:
Pastel swirls, tie dye, dip dye

MOST LIKELY TO...
Dream the day away

YOU'LL FIND HER...
collecting cute manga toys

MOST KNOWN FOR:
Her fluffy bear, crazy coloured hair and, jewel embellished shoes

GIVE THESE PIECES A CANDY-COLOURED TWIST!

CUTE TOYS

DITZY SKIRTS

LEGGINGS

SWEET SHOES

15

GOT UR BACK GRL!

So, Uptown has THE most impeccable manners, and she's learned a thing or two about being a fierce BF. Her all-time bestie Downtown can vouch for that! Take a few of her tips and see your friendships flourish, too.

Uptown's 5 point plan to stay BFs 4life

1. Talk… and listen!

If you're the person that everyone tells their deepest secrets to, then congratulations, you're already on your way to being a fierce and fabulous BF. Listening is as important as chatting, so take time to really hear the things your friends are telling you. You'll become even closer for it.

I listened by…

_____

_____

_____

_____

2. Laugh every day

So you already know that you're gonna stay tight 4eva, because she gets you like no one else does, right? You have your in jokes and the stuff that makes you laugh… these are the things that help people stay BFFs forever! So be sure to take an interest in what makes her laugh, and she'll do the same for you!

What really makes my BFF laugh is…

_____

_____

_____

3. Plan… and plan big!

Thinking ahead can really bring you together, so whether you're thinking about your first apartment together, or that trip to the mall next month, make sure you include her in all your plans. Even if your dreams seem far off, planning them together will help you feel one step closer to achieving them!

We are planning…

_____
_____
_____
_____

4. Be honest and trustworthy…always

So, don't talk behind your friend's back, or say stuff you wouldn't say to her face. Trust is the foundation of all good friendships, and if you're constantly questioning your BF what they're really thinking, you have some friendship work to do! True BFF's always have each others' back and keep it real with trust and honesty.

Can you be trusted?

_____

5. Be kind… and don't sweat the small stuff

Everyone has a down day, and everyone can say stuff they don't really mean at times. But try and remember you do this too, and when you do, you need a friend that's kind and honest. So be that pal right back. Forget about the little niggles and irritations, and focus on what U2 do best… Slaying the runway of life!

I promise to do more of…

_____
_____
_____

SPOTLIGHT ON...

Alt Grrrl

FIERCE, independent and individual!

Alt Grrrl is a little bit outrageous and a whole lot of fierce! Instead of following the style pack, she sets her own rules, ripping up the fashion rules book and rewriting it! She's known for mixing tough poker looks with cute hairstyles, punky with princess... anything goes and she always looks a million dollars.

 SIGNATURE STYLE:
Tartan, safety pins, crystals.

 MOST LIKELY TO...
Rock the front row at the show.

 YOU'LL FIND HER...
Designing her next amazing ensemble.

 MOST KNOWN FOR:
Her bunches, long fringe and biker boots.

ADD A ONE-OFF STYLE TO ALT GRRRL'S NEXT OUTFIT.

HEAVY BOOTS

FRILL SOCKS

PINAFORES

TIES

19

BABYSITTING RULEZZ!

When they're not slaying the runway, the Outrageous Millennial Girls like to teach their LOL sisters their fashion ABC's!

See if you can throw some shade on these two pictures. There are six differences to spot.

Colour in some sunglasses each time you spot something different.

ANSWERS ON PAGE 76

IN THE BAG

Swag is all about the bags. But which one is the odd one out here?

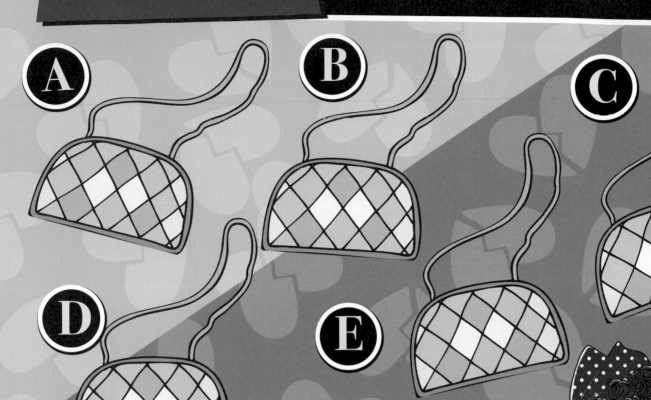

A **B** **C**

D **E**

ALL ABOUT THE YUM YUMS

No babysitting job is complete without some hunger busters! Fill in the missing letters to reveal the OMG's sweetest treat!

POP C ORN   SNAC K S

ICE CRE A M   SWE E TS

ANSWER _ _ _ _

ANSWERS ON PAGE 76

© MGA

21

SIX WAYS TO STAY
OUTRAGEOUS 4 LIFE

Let's get started and slay the Outrageous Millennial Girl way!

CHANGE UP THE VIBE

Not loving your latest look? Not feeling your latest project? Channel the Outrageous Millennial Girls and don't be afraid to start it all over. In fact, sometimes, that's where their best ideas come from. Mashing the old with the new always makes for an exciting new trend!

MY CREW IS FIERCE

The Outrageous Millennial Girls stand together, no matter what. They support each others' projects and celebrate every fashion victory, together. Treating your friends like queens is what they're all about!

I GOT MAD SWAG

They have magnetic personalities and everyone wants to be around the Outrageous Millennial Girls! Whether they're collaborating on a new design project, or DJ-ing at the club, you can spot them by their positive attitude, and confident swagger.

GOT NOTHIN' TO PROVE

The Outrageous Millennial Girls can do 'tude is takes them places, and they never worry about what others think. They just keep on plugging away until they achieve their dreams - their goals, their terms!

STRENGTH OF A QUEEN

Being their best every day is a talent that comes naturally to an Outrageous Millennial Girl. They're never gonna give up until all their goals are slayed, and neither should you! So go for it, these girls have your back!

FIERCE, FLAWLESS FABULOUS

It's a mindset, not a look! The Outrageous Millennial Girls believe in themselves, and they love to express their personalities through fashion and all-round fabulousness. Taking time to feel good on the inside means they're always looking good on the outside.

SPOTLIGHT ON...

Cosmic Nova

Dreamy, sweet with a fun fashion **TWIST!**

When she's not busy stargazing or cracking open the secrets of the universe, Cosmic Nova is one stylish BB! She brings a sparkling and sassy twist to all of her looks, choosing deep purples, blues and crystal sparkles. All the colours of the milky way!

 **SIGNATURE STYLE:**
Purple, sparkles, fringing.

 **MOST LIKELY TO...**
Discover a new planet.

 **YOU'LL FIND HER...**
Holding her own art exhibition, all about space!

 **MOST KNOWN FOR:**
Multiple bunches, big earrings, cool hats.

ADD SOME COWGIRL STYLE TO COSMIC NOVA'S NEXT DREAMY LOOK.

COWBOY HATS

FAKE FURS

DISCOBALL BAG

GLITTER HEELS

SHOUT OUT TO MY GIRLS

Nothing says it better than a SLOGAN TEE!

Say it, and say it LOUD with a slogan tee. Choose a shout out from the list, then add it to each girl's tee for some fierce style!

We so surprising
Takin' on the world
Let's go!
We so rockin'
We so outrageous
We groove
Got nothin' to prove
Me and my crew
I'm with my crew
We ride
We're gonna
Slay all day

Lady Diva slogan style:
CHOOSE SOMETHING FIERCE

Don't forget to add some crazy colour, too.

Busy B.B.
Slogan style:
CHOOSE SOMETHING FABULOUS

Cosmic Nova slogan style:
CHOOSE SOMETHING FLAWLESS

A DAY IN THE LIFE
OF DOWNTOWN B.B.

7am Starting the day as I mean to go on - fierce and fabulous! So that's straight to an early morning dance class to bust some moves and bring the positive vibe!

9am Breakfast meeting! I'm working on my insta feed with my friend, Lady Diva. So many people want to know where we get our street style ideas! Power up with a berry smoothie and a breakfast burrito.

10am Hop on the subway to meet an up and coming fashion designer. Our latest collab is a camo collection with sparkling crystal embellishments. We get all our ideas from cool girls we see on the street.

THIS GIRL SLAYS ALL DAY AND PARTIES ALL NIGHT!

12pm It's an early lunch on the go, while cruising the store fronts for fashion inspiration. Alt Grrrl's keeping me company! Mixing high end fashion with street style is our go-to look, every time.

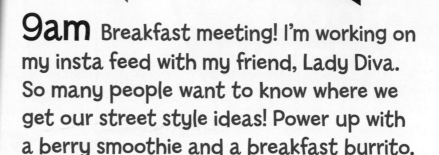

2pm Keeping my tresses true blue is a full time job, so I breeze over to my stylist's super-cool salon for a colour top up. He's a stylist to the stars, and I catch some top showbiz gossip. Shhh!

4pm A fashion editor wants to see me, so I dash to her office for a go-see. She's recruiting for a hot fashion show, and she knows I can slay the runway like no other!

5pm Brush up on my life drawing skills at my art class. I'm fashion through and through, and my teacher is helping me with my sketching.

7pm No time for dinner, 'cos I'm dropping some big beats at a party across town. Meet 24K D.J. on the way, and we firm up our playlist. Getting loud, music pumpin'!

12am Woah, that was some party, and who would have thought that some big name pop stars would swing by too! Shattered, but ready for another big day tomorrow. That's just how we do!

SPOTLIGHT ON...

Busy B.B.

Wholesome...with a **DASH OF FIERCE!**

Busy B.B. is a jeans and plaid shirt kinda gal, and laid back cool is her fashion superpower. No outfit is complete without her signature, oversized bow, and she finishes her look with colour-poppin' work boots.

SIGNATURE STYLE:
Denim, denim and more denim!

MOST LIKELY TO...
Fix your sports car.

YOU'LL FIND HER...
Designing sets for fashion and rock shows.

MOST KNOWN FOR:
Bows and hoop earrings.

ADD SOME SASS TO BUSY B.B.'S FAVOURITE DENIM PIECES

JACKET

BOWS

JEANS

DUNGAREES

© MGA

31

What's your PERFECT *Nail vibe?*

Choose your fabulous fashion accessories and we'll reveal your best nail life!

Tick one accessory for each question, then nail your next manicure move!

1 GRAB A BAG:

A **B** **C** **D**

2 WHOSE HAIR ARE YOU LOVING?

 **A**  **B**  **C**  **D**

3 LISTEN UP! WHICH EARRINGS?

A **B** **C** **D**

④ BEST FOOT FORWARD... CHOOSE A SHOE.

Ⓐ  Ⓑ  Ⓒ  Ⓓ

⑤ WHICH NECKLACE WILL YOU SLAY TODAY?

Ⓐ Ⓑ Ⓒ Ⓓ

    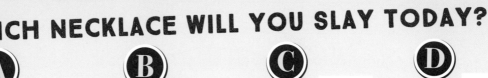 

Now add up

YOUR ANSWERS

and have your nails at the ready!

MOSTLY A	MOSTLY B	MOSTLY C	MOSTLY D

You like to mix and match our styles, so go for a zig-zag mani, like this one. You'll be runway ready, whatever the day brings!	It's all about the detail for you, so go for a mani to match! Take your time with this polka dot perfection. It will take a bit of planning, but will be so worth it.	You're all about making bold statements. This heart-embellished manicure will take you from day to night and is sure to get you pitied in all the right ways.	Colour-popping styles help you slay every day, so match your outfits with this neon manicure. There's no such thing as too much colour!

HAIR-MAZING

You don't need much to experiment with a new hairstyle, just a few clips and a big imagination!

You'll need:
- Brush
- 4 x hair ties
- Comb
- Kirby grips

HIGH BUNS

⭐ First, brush your hair and separate into two bunches. Brush them upwards, to make two high pony-tails, and secure with a hair tie.

⭐ Using your comb, lightly backcomb the hair to make it go large! Then arrange each bunch into a bun shape.

⭐ Use your other hair tie to secure the bun, and use your kirby grips to tuck away any messy ends.

CLIP CRAZY

⭐ Brush your hair, and make a parting just to the side

⭐ Set your style with a little spray.

⭐ Sweep your fringe across your forehead, then carefully place your clip in the side.

You'll need:
- Brush
- Styling spray
- Your favourite clips

You'll need:
- Brush
- Styling spray
- Lots of hair bands

PLAITS, PLEASE

⭐ Brush your hair, then section it according to how many braids you'd like.

⭐ Now for the fun bit! Carefully plait each braid, then secure with a hair band.

⭐ Spray each braid as it's finished, to keep each one neat.

⭐ Repeat with each section, until all your sections are braided.

SPOTLIGHT ON...

Neonlicious

A colour-poppin' show-stoppin' fashion **QUEEN!**

Neonlicious is all about the quirk - think cute handbags, jaunty hats and one-off cropped jackets. Somehow she pulls it all together into a total fashion dream of eye popping colour. But you can't copy this fierce fashionista - she customises everything so she can't be copied!

 **SIGNATURE STYLE:**
Brights, cutesy accessories, platform boots.

 **MOST LIKELY TO...**
Customise everything she gets her hands on.

 **YOU'LL FIND HER...**
Trailblazing in the front row of fashion week.

 **MOST KNOWN FOR:**
Leopard print and big earrings.

TURN UP THE BRIGHTNESS FOR NEONLICIOUS.

BERETS

SKIRTS

CUTE BAGS

PLATFORMS

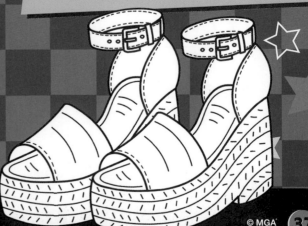

24K D.J. IN THE HOUSE!

Everyone's favourite Outrageous Millennial Girl is on the decks tonight.

It's an all night long kinda vibe and 24K has the tunes that rock da house!

How many music words can you find in the grid?

F	J	O	X	K	X	X	P	N	R	H	E	W	B	L	W	F
H	W	R	E	F	S	S	R	Y	P	F	L	U	X	E	S	M
X	G	E	G	H	M	E	W	U	O	W	B	T	S	E	T	C
N	C	M	Y	I	R	N	D	A	V	X	A	B	V	E	V	D
V	V	I	E	W	S	O	V	U	W	K	T	B	M	J	A	T
W	X	X	U	T	L	H	W	G	S	T	N	D	A	N	V	M
L	C	G	Q	T	R	P	I	G	P	I	R	R	C	G	N	O
D	F	C	E	G	Q	D	W	K	P	U	U	E	I	Z	J	W
K	G	V	Y	E	E	A	Z	T	C	A	T	I	Y	O	M	P
Z	R	Z	Z	T	T	E	J	E	J	O	I	S	K	I	L	U
S	R	L	A	F	E	H	K	B	D	R	R	R	V	C	C	M
O	E	P	G	G	U	E	G	M	E	S	O	D	J	R	O	I
G	W	V	M	P	L	R	O	R	G	A	G	W	G	E	R	S
N	O	G	O	K	N	J	K	V	O	N	T	W	X	W	R	M
N	N	W	B	M	D	Q	Z	C	J	O	O	J	N	C	Y	I
T	J	D	E	L	T	R	J	W	C	M	V	D	Q	F	M	E
F	H	H	X	Y	H	Q	C	B	V	S	U	E	D	O	Q	N

TURNTABLE   **ROCK**   **BEAT**   **MOVES**   **SET**

REMIX   **GROOVE**   **CREW**   **HEADPHONES**   **DANCE**

ANSWERS ON PAGE 76

TOTAL FAIL!

The girls' insta feed is on the fritz! Can you tell who each character is?

a

b

c

d

LADY DIVA

PHONE ⊘

MISS INDEPENDENT

PHONE ⊘

SHADOW

PHONE ⊘

BUSY B.B.

PHONE ⊘

ANSWERS ON PAGE 76

© MGA

39

LET'S FACE IT

Get an Outrageous Millennial Girl glow for next to nothing!

HOMEMADE FACE MASK

ALL YOU NEED
- 1 egg yolk
- 1 teaspoon of olive oil
- 1 tablespoon of honey

MAKE IT
1. Mix all the ingredients and apply to your clean face.
2. Leave for 15 minutes.
3. Wash off, pat dry and apply some moisturiser.
4. Ta da! Super soft skin!

HEAVENLY HAIR

ALL YOU NEED
- One egg (two for long hair)

MAKE IT
1. Beat the egg(s) in a mixing bowl.
2. Massage the mixture into your dry hair and leave for five minutes.
3. Rinse your hair thoroughly in cool water.
4. Condition and style as normal (or use the mayonnaise recipe below).

These recipes may contain ingredients that some readers could be allergic to. Check with a grown-up first.

MARVELLOUS MAYO CONDITIONER

MAKE IT

1. Smooth a good dollop of mayonnaise onto clean, wet hair.
2. Leave it on for five minutes, then rinse it out.
3. Dry your hair and - voila - you have beautiful, shiny mane of hair.

Hellooo gorgeous!

LUSCIOUS LIP BALM

ALL YOU NEED
- Vaseline
- Different shades of lipstick
- A small container

MAKE IT

1. Put a large blob of vaseline on you hand, then mix in the lipstick.
2. Keep adding colour until you get a shade you like and the mixture is nice and soft.
3. Scoop the mixture off your hand into a container.
4. Hey presto - instant lip balm! Plus no one else in the world will have the exact, same shade as you!

FABULOUS FOOT SCRUB

ALL YOU NEED
- 2 bananas
- 2 tablespoons of sugar
- Warm milk

ASK A GROWN-UP FOR HELP BEFORE HEATING THE MILK.

MAKE IT

1. Mash up the bananas with the sugar.
2. Gradually stir in a cup of warm milk.
3. Rub on your feet like you would moisturiser.
4. After three minutes, rinse your feet with warm water and dry them.
5. Paint your toe nails, and you'll not only have gorgeous-smelling, but gorgeous-looking tootsies!

© MGA

SPOTLIGHT ON...

Uptown B.B.

Meet the **FIERCE, FAB AND FUN GIRL** who always brings it.

Sometimes a little girly. Sometimes a little extra, Uptown B.B. always has a fresh and totally immaculate take on tailored prints mixed with boucle. You can be sure you'll never ever see her with a single perfectly pink hair even slightly out of place. Her accessories are always gorgeously on point from pearl hair clips, to Designer bags.

 SIGNATURE STYLE:
Fierce and fun.

 MOST LIKELY TO...
Go designer shopping.

 YOU'LL FIND HER...
Customising her fashion looks with clips and belts, while applying lip gloss.

 MOST KNOWN FOR:
Incredible bag collection, designer of course.

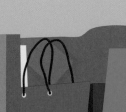

WHAT AN AMAZING HAUL.
DOODLE A DESIGNER
LOGO ON UPTOWN'S
SHOPPING BAGS.

43

Never TOO EXTRA

The Outrageous Millennial Girls know you can never have too many accessories. Doodle more show-stoppin' must-haves here.

SPOTLIGHT ON...
24K D.J.

24K D.J. KILLS IT EVERY DAY when it comes to fashion and music

DRAW A VINYL SLEEVE FOR YOUR FAVOURITE RECORD ARTIST SO D.J. CAN ROCK THE DANCE FLOOR.

This girl really knows how to work flawless street style with metallic bomber jackets, luxe lounge wear matched with gold boots and always with her signature head phones firmly in place. From her vinyl bag packed with the latest tunes to her gold boots, 24K D.J. rocks every joint in town.

SIGNATURE STYLE:
Street meets luxe.

MOST LIKELY TO...
Dance like no B.B. is watchin'.

YOU'LL FIND HER...
Filling every dance floor with her outrageously-good tunes.

MOST KNOWN FOR:
Her signature gold headphones.

FASHION FORTUNES

Find out what's in your fashion stars!

ARIES
March 21 – April 20

Watch out world. You are ready to slay all day this year and you're going to blow everyone's fashionable socks off.

LUCKY CHARM: White sunglasses
LUCKY COLOUR: Blue
LUCKY MONTH: October
MOTTO FOR THE YEAR: Rock star

TAURUS
April 21 – May 21

Your fashion smarts will be on full display this year. In fact your style grades will be the highest they've ever been.

LUCKY CHARM: A necklace with your initial on
LUCKY COLOUR: Red
LUCKY MONTH: February
MOTTO FOR THE YEAR: Stand out from the crowd!

LEO
July 23 – August 23

This will be your happiest and most stylish year. It's the start of a new adventure for you and your BFFs.

LUCKY CHARM: A silver bracelet
LUCKY COLOUR: Purple
LUCKY MONTH: December
MOTTO FOR THE YEAR: Create your own buzz!

VIRGO
August 24 – September 22

Want to know why this is such a great year for you? Because you'll meet someone who loves fashion as much as you!

LUCKY CHARM: A gold ring
LUCKY COLOUR: Yellow
LUCKY MONTH: January
MOTTO FOR THE YEAR: I got mad swag!

SAGITTARIUS
November 23 – December 21

You'll find yourself discovering more ways to rewear your wardrobe. Fab, because rewear is the best wear!

LUCKY CHARM: A jeweled charm
LUCKY COLOUR: Green
LUCKY MONTH: July
MOTTO FOR THE YEAR: Got nothin' to prove!

CAPRICORN
December 22 – January 20

The stars will align and you'll feel better than you've ever felt about your sense of style. Positive vibes!

LUCKY CHARM: A gold bangle
LUCKY COLOUR: Grey
LUCKY MONTH: May
MOTTO FOR THE YEAR: Diva 4 life

GEMINI

May 22 – June 21

If there's one fashion word that's important to you it's 'fabulous'. Your look will be off the hook.

LUCKY CHARM: A patterned scarf
LUCKY COLOUR: Orange
LUCKY MONTH: June
MOTTO FOR THE YEAR: Strut ur stuff!

CANCER

June 22 – July 22

Check you out, Miss Fierce. At the end of the year, you'll impress people with your flawless customising skills.

LUCKY CHARM: A pair of white shoes
LUCKY COLOUR: White
LUCKY MONTH: April
MOTTO FOR THE YEAR: Misson 2 glam!

LIBRA

September 23 – October 23

You'll show your stuff this year when you're faced with a serious challenge. It won't get you hot under your oh-so-now collar though.

LUCKY CHARM: A distressed pair of jeans
LUCKY COLOUR: Turquoise
LUCKY MONTH: October
MOTTO FOR THE YEAR: I'm extra, very extra!

SCORPIO

October 24 – November 22

You're a busy girl and loving it. Your friends will come to you for fashion advice, and you'll be only too happy to give it.

LUCKY CHARM: A red bag
LUCKY COLOUR: Pink
LUCKY MONTH: April
MOTTO FOR THE YEAR: U glow girl!

AQUARIUS

January 21 – February 18

You'll discover a brand new passion for fashion. We predict it's something to do with denim. You glow girl!

LUCKY CHARM: Neon nail varnish
LUCKY COLOUR: Black
LUCKY MONTH: September
MOTTO FOR THE YEAR: Funk 'n' Shine

PISCES

February 19 – March 20

There'll be nothing reserved about your look. You'll totally put your style out there and make some new fashion friends.

LUCKY CHARM: A pink purse
LUCKY COLOUR: Apricot
LUCKY MONTH: August
MOTTO FOR THE YEAR: With my crew!

MAKE 2021 TOTALLY OUTRAGEOUS

Rule the world in 2021. Fill in a challenge for each month. Make it whatever you want, but make it fierce!

JANUARY

FEBRUARY

MARCH

APRIL

MAY

JUNE

JULY

AUGUST

SEPTEMBER

OCTOBER

NOVEMBER

DECEMBER

SPOTLIGHT ON...

Shadow

A little bit **PUNK**, a little bit **GLAM** Shadow flawlessly mixes it up!

JUST MAKE IT AS ONE-OF-A-KIND AS SHADOW HERSELF.

YOU CAN ACCESSORISE IT WITH SAFETY PINS, RIPS, WHATEVER YOU LIKE.

DRAW A PUNK SLOGAN ON SHADOW'S NEW TEE.

You'll always recognise Shadow by her bright blue hair topped with her trademark baker boy cap and finished off with the most stylish Creepers in town. She mixes blues, blacks with bright pops of purple to create a look that's totally her own.

SIGNATURE STYLE:
Cool with a punk edge.

MOST LIKELY TO...
Wear safety pins in her clothes.

YOU'LL FIND HER...
Flipping through vinyl in a music shop.

MOST KNOWN FOR:
Her amazing collection of boots.

DANCE OFF

Dollie can't wait to boogie at the Winter Disco. Help her come up with some different dance styles so she can slay all day (and all night!).

Fit the dance words into the grid. Tick them off as you find them.

©MGA

©MGA

TANGO ☐ DISCO ☐ TAP ☐ BALLET ☐ SALSA ☐

BREAKDANCE ☐ BALLROOM ☐ HIP HOP ☐ BOLLYWOOD ☐

ANSWER ON PAGE 77

© MGA

GET SASSY

Which fierce saying is for you? Find out right here, right now…

STRUTTIN' SIDE-BY-SIDE

Let's go!

TAKIN' ON THE WORLD

LET'S GET LOUD

Hey Yay!

ME AND MY CREW

GOT NOTHIN' TO PROVE

Break the rules, go against the crowd

I'm wit my crew

WHAT TO DO

1. STARE AT THE PAGE FOR 10 SECONDS.
2. CLOSE YOUR EYES AND REPEAT THIS RHYME "OMG OMG! Which of these sayings is oh so me?"
3. KEEPING YOUR EYES SHUT, MOVE YOUR INDEX FINGER OVER THE SAYINGS THREE TIMES. THEN LET IT DROP.
4. WHEREVER IT LANDS IS YOUR OUTRAGEOUS MILLENNIAL GIRL SIGNATURE SAYING!

© MGA

55

THAT'S SHOE-BUSINESS

Every gal knows you can never have too many shoes.

Add some finishing touches to this gorgeous lot of flawless footwear!

© MGA

WHOSE SHOES?

This crew know how to thrill from head to toe. Can you name each doll just from their fierce foot-wear?

a THIS DOLL STRUTS FASHION, BABY, CUZ SHE WAS BORN A STAR.

THESE GORGEOUS SHOES BELONG TO _____

b THIS IS THE BADDEST M.C. ON THE BLOCK CUZ SHE'S GOT MAD SWAG.

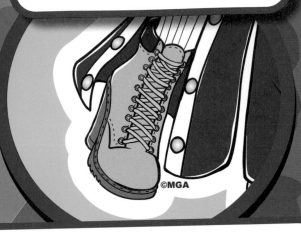

©MGA

THESE HOT-TO-DROP SHOES BELONG TO _____

c THIS GIRL MIXES, MATCHES AND VIBES BRIGHT COLOURS 24/7.

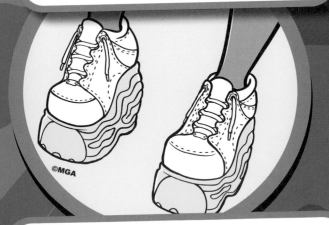

©MGA

THESE GLAM SHOES BELONG TO _____

d SHE RUNS THE WORLD. EVEN WHEN YOU CAN'T SEE HER SHOES, YOU KNOW THEY BRING THE BUZZ!

IF YOU COULD ACTUALLY SEE THESE SHOES THEY WOULD BELONG TO _____

ANSWER ON PAGE 77

LOOK BOOK

Fill this page with the hottest inspiration that will take you from breakfast to the after party!

Fill these with swatches of material that you just gotta have!

© MGA

My favourite looks from the 'gram and magazines etc.

Style I just wanna copy!

My most-wanted items this year!

SPOTLIGHT ON...

Miss Independent

This girl is never ever afraid to **STAND UP OR OUT!**

CREATE SOME NEW HAIRSTYLES FOR MISS INDEPENDENT. MAKE THEM AS FIERCE AS SHE IS.

Move over Beyoncé, there's a new queen in town. This girl is never afraid to stand up for what she believes in and does it while looking absolutely flawless. She mixes denim with sequins and over-the-knee boots to create a trend-setting look that everyone wants to follow.

SIGNATURE STYLE:
Denim with attitude.

MOST LIKELY TO...
Set a new trend.

YOU'LL FIND HER...
In glam. That trademark full blue ponytail takes time, y'know.

MOST KNOWN FOR:
Paying her own way and standing up for what she believes.

SIGNATURE STYLE

Find out what your signature reveals about your Outrageous Millennial Girl fashion profile.

FIRST SIGN YOUR NAME HERE.

WHERE YOU SIGNED IN THE SPACE SHOWS YOUR SWEATER STYLE!

A NEAR THE TOP

You're practical and like to think ahead. You always bring a sweater in case the weather changes just like Snowlicious.

B IN THE CENTRE

You like to be the centre of attention. You'd rather not wear a sweater, but when you do, it'll have sparkles on it just like Crystal Star.

C NEAR THE BOTTOM

You prefer to comfy glam. You like snuggly sweaters with sleeves that flop over your hands. Just like Cosmic Nova.

© MGA

HOW EASY IT IS TO READ YOUR SIGNATURE REVEALS HOW YOU LIKE TO WEAR TOPS!

A SUPER EASY

You don't mind if everyone knows all about your life. You like wearing t-shirts with funny slogans on the front. Alt Grrrl likes your style!

B YOU CAN READ PART OF YOUR NAME

You love gossiping with pals, but don't like your business being broadcast. You like tops you can button up, just like Busy B.B.

C YOU CAN'T READ IT

You're a very private person. You're most at home in hoodies - with the hood up. You and Swag know how to work those track tops.

THE DIRECTION YOUR SIGNATURE SLANTS IN SHOWS YOUR FAVOURITE TYPE OF OUTFIT!

A IT SLANTS FORWARDS TO THE RIGHT.

You're modest and a little shy at times. You prefer long pants and flowy skirts, but like Royal Bee you always create a buzz!

B IT SLANTS BACKWARDS TO THE LEFT.

You're totally comfortable with yourself. You're happy in anything from a mini to a onesie. Whatever you're in, just like Candylicious you rock it.

C SLANT? WHAT SLANT? IT GOES STRAIGHT UP AND DOWN.

You like drawing all eyes to you. You love wearing tights or leggings in crazy patterns. You and Neonlicious are total style twins.

SPOTLIGHT ON...

Downtown B.B.

Whatever her mood, Downtown always looks **FABULOUS**.

DOWNTOWN LOVES BEING DIFFERENT – SHE KNOWS IT'S WHAT MAKES HER SO FIERCE. WRITE A LIST OF WHAT MAKES YOU SO FABULOUSLY UNIQUE HERE.

Downtown loves camouflage prints, but makes sure she never ever blends in with her surroundings. She cleverly uses bright pops of colour in her clothes, which together with her bright blue hair means she always stands out from the crowd.

 SIGNATURE STYLE: Camouflage that always stands out.

 MOST LIKELY TO... Hang out with her BFF, Uptown Girl.

 YOU'LL FIND HER... Shouting out why different is beautiful.

 MOST KNOWN FOR: Those dazzling, bright blue locks!

I'M DIFFERENT BECAUSE...

DOWNTOWN
SWATCH STITCH

Downtown has left a stylish message for you. Crack her fashionista code to work out what it says.

KEY

& =
C =
E =
F =
I =
L =
N =
R =
T =
U =
Y =

You're

F I E R C E

F L I R T Y

& E U N !

Love
Downtown
xox

ANSWER ON PAGE 77

WHAT'S YOUR GO-TO ACCESSORY

Because every Outrageous Millennial Girl has one.

Stare at the words in the box and underline the one that stands out to you. Then use this word to find out which accessory is your go-to!

No cheating! Cover up the accessories before you play!

ENERGY DANCE POSE Happy

BFFs Style ADVENTURE Star

DANCE

ENERGY

SNEAKERS
You're always on the move. A fab pair of sneakers will see you through posing, talking, and slaying all day.

BALLET PUMPS
You're always making moves on the dance floor and when it comes to trends, ballet pumps would work as hard as yourself.

Happy

GLITTER.
Bring on the glitter that will make you smile, Outrageous Millennial Girl-style.

Star

A BLING BRACELET
After all accessories should be just as fabulous as you are.

ADVENTURE

RUCKSACK
You could travel the world together having all kinds of fierce and fashionable adventures.

POSE

A CAMERA
Perfect to help you create fashion memories. If there's no photo evidence, did it really happen.

BFFs

FRIENDSHIP NECKLACE
A friendship necklace will always remind you of your pals whatever you're up to.

Style

A BAG
Every fashionista knows a great bag never goes out of style.

THE OUTRAGEOUS MILLENNIAL GIRL A-Z

Being outrageous is as easy as ABC!

A is for ALL eyes on you, cuz you lead the fashion pack.

B is for BRINGING the buzz. Outrageous Millennial Girls always know how to work it.

C is for CHILLIN' out with your B.Bs. Still in total style obviously.

D D is for DESIGNED to thrill. No matter where we are.

I is for I did not come here to play! So watch out world.

J is for that's JUST how we do everything. Glow girls!

K is for KICKIN' boring to the kerb. Oh yes.

L is for LOVING and living every fashion and fun-filled minute.

Q is for QUEEN of my own fashion life.

R is for READY for my selfie. Otherwise it didn't happen.

S is for STRUTTIN' your stuff. You were born a fashion star.

T is for THESE kittens have claws. Meow!

E
is for **EXTRA**. Always be extra, but never 2 much!

F
is for **FIERCE**, **FABULOUS** and **FLAWLESS**. Who needs one word when three will do it sooo much better.

G
is for **GLAMOUROUS**. Outrageous Millennial Girls wake up glamorous and fresh every, single day.

H
is for **HEAR** us when we say Oh Yay!

M
is for **MARCHING** to the beat of your own D.J.

N
is for **NEVER** fitting into just one box.

O
is for **OUTRAGEOUS**. We're here to surprise the world.

P
is for **PARTIES** that never end. Fashion is one long party, darlin.

U
is for **UNSTOPPABLE** glam. Oh yes.

V
is for **VIBIN'** rainbow colours 24/7.

W
is for a **WHOLE** lotta funk 'n' shine.

X
is for **X-FACTOR**. All the Outrageous Millennial Girls have it.

Y
is for **YOUR** ticket to the baddest of the bad.

Z
is for **ZZZZ**. Every Outrageous Millennial Girl needs her beauty sleep.

SPOTLIGHT ON...

Royal Bee

BRING THE BUZZ!
Royal Bee runs her fashion world.

DRAW A DAY OUTFIT AND NIGHT OUTFIT FOR ROYAL BEE. THERE'S ONLY ONE RULE, BRING THE GLAMOUR!

DAY

NIGHT

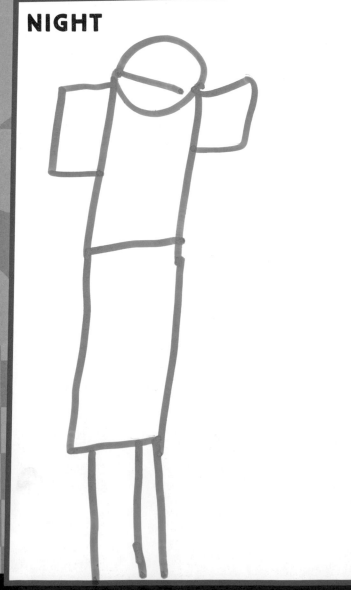

Fierce, fashionable and flawless, this girl wakes up glamorous every day. All her designs are fierce and fresh. Royal Bee has tons of BFFs she hearts and always makes time for her girls so she al-ways has outfits to chill and fashion designs that thrill.

SIGNATURE STYLE:
Fierce glamour that's never intimidating.

MOST LIKELY TO...
Make a buzz, Royal Bee style.

YOU'LL FIND HER...
Surrounded by her BFFs.

MOST KNOWN FOR:
Glamour, glamour and more glamour.

KEEPIN' IT COSY!

Snowlicious knows cold weather is snow joke when it comes to fashion. She always brrrrings it!

Custom doodle fierce patterns on to these sleep masks.

Make this onesie a mash-up blend of fun. You can never be too extra!

Add some cute details to these pyjamas but make it fashion.

© MGA

73

CAN DO DIVA!

Follow Lady Diva's 11 confidence-boosting tips and kill it every day!

1 HAVE FUN WITH YOUR STYLE. YOU'LL BE SURPRISED AT THE SMILES AND COMPLIMENTS YOU GET WHEN YOU JUST OWN IT.

Experiment with different styles and trends. The more you practice, the more confident you become until you're a diva for life. **2**

3 BAD OUTFIT DAY? LESSON LEARNED AND MOVE ON. NEXT TIME YOU'LL SLAY IT.

Remember you don't have to jump on every trend. You're a rock star, so listen to yourself and dare to have your own style.

5 To make your eyelashes extra, very extra, put glitter gel on a clean toothbrush and gently brush on to your lashes.

6 To instantly transform an outfit... all you have to do is add a glam choker or a necklace. Instant Diva vibes.

7 Don't copy others. Develop a look that's totally you and you'll rule the world.

8 Style isn't just about looking good. It's also about feeling good. Time to rock it.

9 Fashion is something you buy. Style is something you have, so dress like no B.B. is watching.

10 A smile is the best accessory to any outfit. Remember to smile whenever you need a fierce confidence boost.

11 U glow girl! Protect your skin! Always wear sunscreen!

PUZZLE ANSWERS

Page 13

Page 20

Page 38

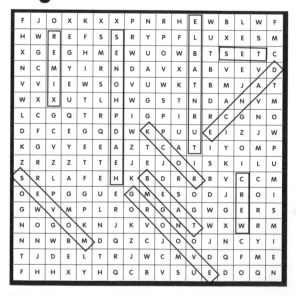

Page 21

IN THE BAG
Bag C is the odd one out

ALL ABOUT THE YUM YUMS
Cake

Page 39

Shadow is phone A

Lady Diva is phone B

Miss Independant is phone C

Busy B.B. is phone D

Page 54

```
        B
    S A L S A          T A P
        L          T A N G O
    B R E A K D A N C E
        E
    B A L L R O O M
        L
    H I P H O P
        Y
        W
        O
        D I S C O
```

Page 57

A - Lady diva

B - Swag

C - Neonlicious

D - Royal Bee

Page 54

Fierce, flirty & fun

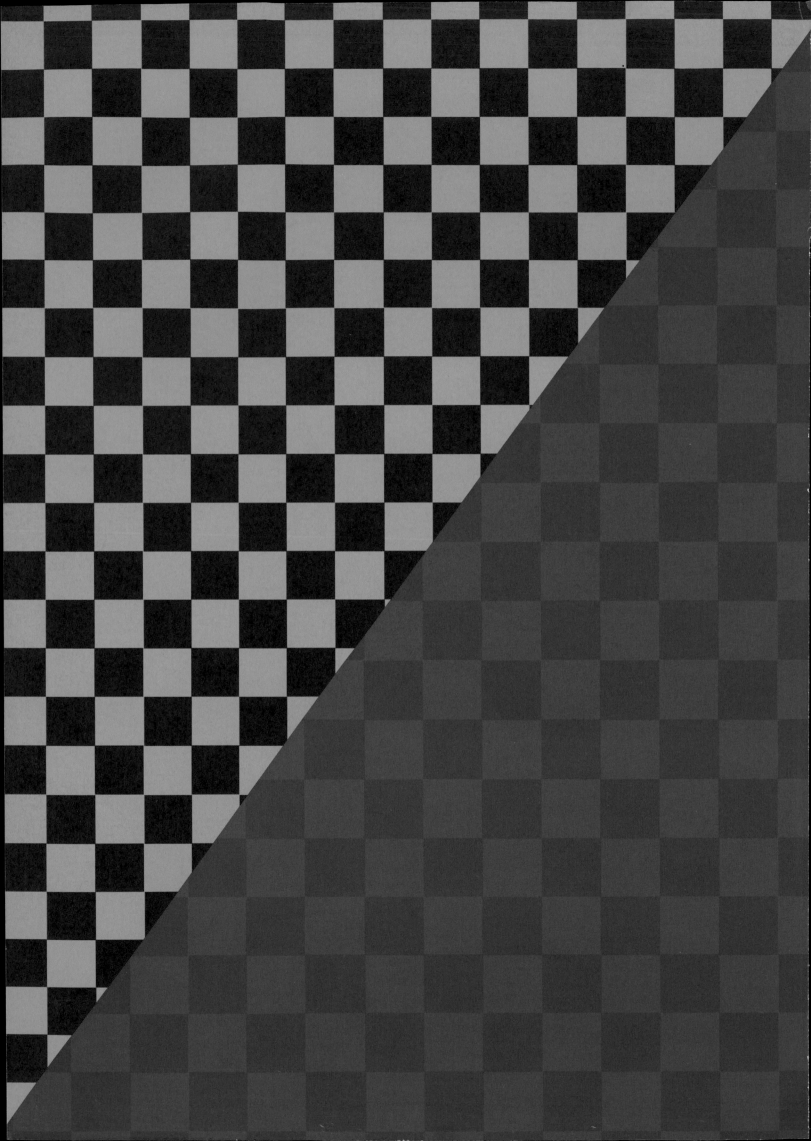